C#

Step-By-Step Guide To C# Programming For Beginners

Robert Anderson

TABLE OF CONTENTS

Chapter 1

Setup and Introduction

History of C#

C# first appeared in 2000 when it was announced by Microsoft, C# is a Microsoft owned language stemming from the C family. It was designed by a team run by Anders Hejlsberg. Initially it proposed the language would be called *"Cool"* standing for *"C-Like Object Orientated Language"* with Microsoft finally deciding to call it C#. The hash symbol is used but pronounced as 'sharp', this was chosen on purpose because of the lack of sharp symbol on many of the keyboards at the time. The sharp symbol also resembles four plus symbols in a 2x2 grid, strongly implying that C# is a later increment of its brother language C++.

Below is a timeline of the C# language and what inclusions each increment added or improved (All features will be explained later in the tutorial):

Jan 2002

C# 1.0

-Type safe programming language

-Modern

-OOP (Object Orientated Programming)

Nov 2005

C# 2005

    -Generics

    -Partial classes

    -Anonymous types

    -Iterators

    -Nullable types

    -Static classes

Nov 2007

C# 2007

    -Improvements of previous additions

    -Extensions methods

    -Expression trees

    -Partial methods

April 2010

C# 4.0

    -Dynamic binding

    -Naming and optional arguments

Aug 2012

C# 5.0

    -Asynchronous Programming

A huge addition allowing programmers to create multithreaded applications

    -Caller info attributes

July 2015

C# 6.0 (Version in this tutorial)

    -Exception filters

    -String interpolation

    -Static type members into namespaces

    -Complier as a service

Why C#?

C# has many advantages over other similar languages like Java and Python.

- C# is incredibly type safe meaning when a variable is created a type must be defined, that means another type cannot be housed in this variable.

- C# has full control over memory leaks that are a big worry for many C++ programmers.

- C# also provides a rich library of features that's allows implementing extra features easy and straightforward

- Any system with the .NET framework will run this application. However, the framework is mainly supported on Windows, meaning Linux and Mac support is thin or entirely non-existent.

Running C# on Windows

Running C# in my opinion is the best way and pretty much only way to code and work with C#, it a Microsoft created language and they have done everything they can to make it easy to work with on a Windows machine, even if it means ignoring other platforms entirely.

Mac Users:

There has recently been a release of Visual Studio for Mac, but it is rudimental and does not have the features that Windows Visual Studio has, it is therefore heavily advised to work with C# on a Windows machine. But, there are ways to have a Windows OS to run on a Mac, look up "Virtual Box" by Oracle, it is a program that allows you to run a virtual Windows machine.

To work with C#, you will need to download **Visual Studio**, it can be downloaded directly from Microsoft. Please run the installer and install Visual Studio.

When you have a fully working instillation you should be greeted with this screen:

Click File and then select "New Project"

You'll be presented with the screen below, select ConsoleApplication and give it a name below:

Click "Ok". You'll then be presented with some code where you'll be ready to program.

Chapter 2

Classes and Object Orientated Programming

Basic classes

Classes are used to store variable and functionality relevant to an object, for example there can be a class created for a 'Book', it would have information such as number of pages, genre and cover colour and functionality like 'loan book' or 'return book'. This is where the whole useful and real world related nature comes from with classes, and the word **object** in the OOP.

Before we go into how to create a class there are accessor keywords that need to be understood:

- private   Cannot be accessed outside the scope of the class

- public   Can be accessed anywhere

- protected   Can be accessed from inherited classes

You define a class like so:

```
class Book
{

}
```

With all its variables and functions defined within the brackets, a fleshed-out version is below:

```
class Book
{
    public Book(int numberOfPages, int currentPage, string colour,
string name)
    {
        _numberOfPages = numberOfPages;
        _currentPage = currentPage;
        _colour = colour;
        _name = name;
    }

    private int _numberOfPages;
    private int _currentPage;
    private string _colour;
    private string _name;

    public string changeMe;

    public int returnCurrentPage()
    {
        return _currentPage;
    }

}
```

There are a few things to note. The function in the box is knowns as a Constructor (Explained in this chapter), it is called when creating a new object. This class contains all the member variables and member functions, they are both accessed by using the member operator (.). In this case all the variables are marked as 'private' meaning they cannot be accessed from outside the class, this is where getters and setters (Accessor methods) come into use, the function 'returnCurrentPage' is a getter and allows access to the currentPage value, this is the recommended way of dealing with variable access, it allows a platform for the programmer to control access to variables.

An object is created below, with some of its functions and variables being accessed:

```
class Program
{
    static void Main(string[] args)
    {
        Book book1 = new Book(200, 32, "Red", "Harry Potter");

        book1.changeMe = "Test";
        Console.WriteLine(book1.changeMe);

        int currentPage = book1.returnCurrentPage();
        Console.WriteLine(currentPage);
    }
}
```

Output
>Test
>32

Recap

- Classes provide an intuitive way to store data on real world objects

- They allow functionality to be built up around the data

- Are used as a cookie-cutter way of making lots of containers for data

- Accessor methods allow access to private variables

    o Getters return the variables value

    o Setters allow to program to change the value

Properties

As mentioned in the previous chapter were Accessor methods, properties allow an easily readable solution to accessing member variables in a tiny compact syntax. Properties also contain the variable definition. They are defined like so:

```
public int currentPage
{
    get
    {
        return currentPage;
    }
    set
    {
        currentPage = value;
    }
}
```

And called like this:

```
Book book1 = new Book();

book1.currentPage = 2; //2 is 'value' in the set
Console.WriteLine(book1.currentPage);
```

This performs exactly the same role as the accessors in the previous chapter but with a much more concise syntax, for comparison:

```
private int _currentPage;
public int returnCurrentPage()
{
        return _currentPage;
}
```

Is equal to:

```
public int currentPage { get; }
```

As you can see it's a much smaller set of code.

A more advanced use of the setter could be to validate the input. For example, you can't have a current page that is larger than the total number of pages. This code could look like this:

```
class Book
{
     int totalPages = 500;
     public int currentPage
     {
        get
        {
           return currentPage;
        }
        set
        {
           //Validation check
           if (value < totalPages)
           {
              currentPage = value;
```

```csharp
            }
            else if(value == totalPages)
            {
                Console.WriteLine("You've finished the book!");
            }
            else
            {
                //Error message
                Console.WriteLine("Invalid current page!");
            }
        }
    }
}
```

This gives the programmer the ability to write code that accounts for many possibilities.

Static

As mentioned in previous chapters member functions allow classes to hold functionality that is somehow related to the data contained within, this allows classes to be almost self-contained programs this along with member variables gives classes their functionality.

Member functions and variables can be defined as 'static', meaning the object is 'always there'. This is used when behaviour will not change between all instances of the class and it means that the behaviour or variable is shared between them all.

Note: static functions can only access static variables

```csharp
using System;

namespace ConsoleApplication1
{
    //
    class Program
    {
        static void Main(string[] args)
        {
            Example e = new Example();
            e.Instance();
            e.Static() //Error

            Example.Instance(); //Error
            Example.Static();
        }
    }

    class Example
    {
```

```
        public void Instance()
        {
            Console.WriteLine("Instance!");
        }
        public static void Static()
        {
            Console.WriteLine("Static!");
        }
    }
}
```

The example above shows how the different types of functions are accessed and dealt with.

Below is an example of static working within a 'real-world' example:

```
using System;

namespace ConsoleApplication1
{
    //
    class Program
    {
        static void Main(string[] args)
        {
            int i = Person.WorkOutAge(new DateTime(1990, 10, 15));
            Console.WriteLine(i);
        }
    }

    class Person
    {
        public Person(string _name, int _age)
        {
```

```csharp
        name = _name;
        age = _age;
    }

    public string name { get; }
    public int age { get; }

    public static int WorkOutAge(DateTime birthday)
    {
        //Time since
        TimeSpan difference = DateTime.Now - birthday;

        double years = difference.TotalDays / 365;

        return (int)years;
    }
  }
}
```

This program uses a static method to work out the age of somebody using their birthday, this allows the method to hold relevant functions without a separate one being created per instance.

Constructors and Destructors

When creating an instance of a class a constructor is used, the language provides a default constructor, but a custom constructor can be created, you may have seen the functions without a return type and with exactly the same name as the class, to continue with our person class example:

```
class Person
{
    public Person()
    {
        Console.WriteLine("Person created");

    }

}
```

This is a custom constructor that just prints when a Person is made. Normally constructors are used to pass in data to member variables when an instance of the class is created.

You can also have as many constructors as you like, however they all need varying parameters types and number of parameters (this is known as a function signature) so with the example above I could not define another constructor with no parameters, this is known as **overloading.**

For example:

```
namespace ConsoleApplication1
{
    class Program
    {
```

```csharp
static void Main(string[] args)
{
    Person p1 = new Person("John", 32);
    Person p2 = new Person("James", 50, "Train Driver");
}
}

class Person
{
    public Person(string _name, int _age)
    {
        name = _name;
        age = _age;
        job = "N/A";
    }
    public Person(string _name, int _age, string _job)
    {
        name = _name;
        age = _age;
        job = _job;
    }

    public string name { get; }
    public int age { get; }
    public string job { get; }

}
}
```

The highlighted sections show the use of the overloading, the compiler automatically detects which constructor to use depending on the types in the parameter list.

Just like the constructor there is a destructor that performs the opposite role of the constructor that instead of dealing with creation code the destructor deals with clean-up code.

A destructor is created like so:

```
class Person
{
    ~Person()
    {
        Console.WriteLine("Person deleted!");
    }
}
```

This method **cannot** be called manually but is managed by the internal Garbage Collector that is a built-in part of the compiler designed for automatic memory management.

This can be demonstrated like this, if a method is called that creates an instance to Person and then the program goes out of scope for the main method the garbage collector will be called to clean up the memory

```csharp
using System;
namespace ConsoleApplication1
{
    class Program
    {
        static void Main(string[] args)
        {
            Function();

        }

        static void Function()
        {
            Person p1 = new Person();
        }
    }

    class Person
    {
        ~Person()
        {
            Console.WriteLine("Person deleted!");
            Console.ReadKey();
        }
    }
}
```

Output
>Person deleted!

Exercise

Create a class that holds data for Pets, the class will need a Name, Age and Type of animal. There also will need to be a Constructor, Destructor and a member function that prints all the data for the pet.

Test it by having a dog called Jose that is 1 year old, A cat called Besse that is 5 and a parrot called James that is 10.

Solution

Something like this:

```
using System;
namespace ConsoleApplication1
{
    class Program
    {
        static void Main(string[] args)
        {
            Pet p1 = new Pet("Jose", 1, "Dog");
            p1.Print();

            Pet p2 = new Pet("Besse", 5, "Cat");
            p2.Print();

            Pet p3 = new Pet("James", 10, "Parrot");
            p3.Print();

            Console.ReadKey();
        }
    }
}
```

```csharp
class Pet
{
    public Pet(string _name, int _age, string _type)
    {
        name = _name;
        age = _age;
        type = _type;
    }

    string name { get; }
    int age { get; }
    string type { get; }

    public void Print()
    {
        // {name} is string interpolation
        Console.WriteLine($"Name:   {name}",name);
        Console.WriteLine($"Age:    {age}",age);
        Console.WriteLine($"Type:   {type}",type);
        Console.WriteLine();
    }
}
}
```

Inheritance

Inheritance is a language function that allows classes to take on characteristics of another, inheritance is done like so:

```
class Dog : Animal
{

}
```

This means that any function or variable marked as "Public" or "Protected" (Protected is explained in the next chapter) Dog will have its own version of or access to, this allows quick creation of new types of classes without having to repeat function and variable definitions.

The example below should how it can be used:

```
using System;
namespace ConsoleApplication1
{
    class Program
    {
        static void Main(string[] args)
        {
            Dog d1 = new Dog("Rocko", 3, "Blue One", "Red");

            d1.PrintName();
        }
    }

    class Animal
    {
        public Animal(string _name, int _age)
```

```
        {
            name = _name;
            age = _age;
        }

        public string name;
        public int age;

        public void PrintName()
        {
            Console.WriteLine(name);
        }
    }

    class Dog : Animal
    {
        public Dog(string _name, int _age, string favBone, string kColour) :
base(_name, _age)
        {
            FavouriteBone = favBone;
            kColour = KennelColour;
        }

        private string FavouriteBone;
        private string KennelColour;
    }
}
```

There are a few points to mention, the first is the example showing how functions are inherited, Dog does not have a definition for "PrintName" but because it inherits "Animal" it has its own definition.

The other point it is the "base(_name, _age)", this is how you call the base constructor, in this case it's calling the Animal constructor above.

Encapsulation

Encapsulating is the process of enclosing one or more items within a physical or logical package and in the context of OOP is how access to member variables is managed.

We've seen three of these before but this section will go into more detail about the sections below:

- Public

- Protected

- Private

- Internal

- Protected internal

Public

Public simply allows full access to all member objects.

For example:

```
class Program
{
    static void Main(string[] args)
    {
        Public p = new Public();

        //value can be accessed and changed no problem
        p.value = 3;
    }
}

class Public
{
    public int value;
}
```

Private

Is the complete opposite of public where on internal calls to a variable are allowed, this means if we want to change variable we need to use accessor function:

```
class Program
{
    static void Main(string[] args)
    {
        Private p = new Private();
```

```
        //Error here!
        p.value = 3;
      }
}

class Private
{
    private int value;
}
```

Protected

Protected is a little different, protected involves inheritance is when a class inherits functions and variable from another (Mentioned previously).

Internal

This allows a class to exposed both member functions and variables to objects in the current assembly, essentially this is just any functions contained within the application (.exe or .dll)

Protected Internal

Protected internal is very like internal but with a few differences, it does involve inheritance much like protected.

Note:

You may be thinking what if an access modifier isn't specified? Well, If that is the case (and it's completely valid), it will default to **private**.

End of chapter Quiz

1. What does OOP stand for?

2. What are functions called that allow changes to be made to private member variables?

3. Explain the role of a property?

4. Defining a classes member variable as 'static' achieves what?

5. What can a static function only access?

6. How is the destructor called by the programmer?

7. What section of the complier automatically deals with memory management?

8. Where can you access a variable marked as internal?

9. What is the technical name for a newly created version of a class?

10. What is the name for the use of multiple constructors?

Answers

1. Object Orientated Programming.

2. Getters (Accessor functions).

3. A small more concise syntax for getter, setters and variable definition.

4. This means the variables presence is constant between every instance of the class.

5. Static variables.

6. It is not, the destructor cannot be manually called.

7. The garbage collector

8. In the same assembly, i.e. in the same .exe file or .dll

9. An instance of a class

10. Overloading a class

Chapter 3

Advanced Class structures

Polymorphism

The word polymorphism means having many forms, in the context of OOP is often described as "one interface, many functions".

There are two types of polymorphic design, **static** and **dynamic** polymorphism.

Static Polymorphism

Static polymorphism means the response to a function is determined at compile time (i.e. before the program is run), this process is called 'Early binding' and this can be done in one of two ways:

- Function overloading

- Operator overloading

Function overloading

In function overloading you can have the same definition of a function is the same scope, this is exactly the same to constructor overloading.

So, for example, this class definition would be valid:

```
using System;
namespace ConsoleApplication1
{
```

```csharp
class Program
{
    static void Main(string[] args)
    {
        Interface i = new Interface();

        //Printing integer
        i.Print(1);

        //Printing float
        i.Print(2.0f);

        //Printing double
        i.Print(4d);

        //Printing long
        i.Print(4L);
    }
}

class Interface
{
    string printStr = "Print!";

    public void Print(int i)
    {
        Console.WriteLine(i);
    }

    public void Print(double i)
    {
        Console.WriteLine(i);
    }

    public void Print(float i)
    {
```

```
        Console.WriteLine(i);
    }

    public void Print(long i)
    {
        Console.WriteLine(i);
    }
  }
}
```

As you can tell there are 4 definitions of "Print()" but all with different parameters.

Dynamic overloading

C# allows the creation of an abstract class; an abstract class can act as a template or a design for other classes to inherit and adapt for the circumstance they are designed for. Derived classes then can take abstract functions and adapt their behaviour, however they're some rules about abstract classes:

- You cannot directly create an instance of an abstract class

- You cannot declare an abstract method that is not housed in an abstract class

- There is also a keyword known as **'sealed'** and sealed classes cannot be inherited, abstract methods therefore cannot be defined as sealed

Below is an example that demonstrates the use of an abstract class:

```csharp
using System;
namespace ConsoleApplication1
{
    abstract class Shape
    {
        public abstract int Volume();

        public int height { get; set; }
        public int width { get; set; }
    }

    //Creates a 2D Rectangle
    class Rectangle : Shape
    {
        public Rectangle(int w, int h)
        {
            height = h;
            width = w;
        }

        public override int Volume()
        {
            return height * width;
        }
    }

    //Creates a 3D Cylinder
    class Cylinder : Shape
    {
        public Cylinder(int w, int h)
        {
            height = h;
            width = w;
        }
```

```
    public override int Volume()
    {
        //(π * (width / 2)^3) * height
        return (int)(Math.PI * Math.Pow(width / 2, 3)) * height;
    }
}

class Program
{
    static void Main(string[] args)
    {
        Rectangle rec = new Rectangle(10, 10);
        Console.WriteLine(rec.Volume());

        Cylinder cylin = new Cylinder(10, 10);
        Console.WriteLine(cylin.Volume());

        Console.ReadKey();
    }
}
}
```

A few things to note in this, the area surrounded by the rectangle is the abstract class definition, where an abstract Volume() class is defined, this is then taken in the other methods and **overloaded,** notice the 'overload' keyword that is used to create a custom definition of Volume() where each class has a custom design for Volume that is then called in the Main method. An abstract class requires that the method that inherits it has to create an overloaded version. This means abstract classes are designed to be very strict plans for the shape and layout of a method.

There is also another type of dynamic overloading, it is known as a 'Virtual' this is very similar to abstract but is an optional version, where a definition is

the base class can optionally be overridden, below is an example:

```csharp
using System;
namespace ConsoleApplication1
{
    class Human
    {
        public virtual void SayHello()
        {
            Console.WriteLine("Hello!");
        }
    }

    class American : Human
    {
        //No override needed as SayHello is valid
    }

    class Columbian : Human
    {
        public override void SayHello()
        {
            Console.WriteLine("Hola!");
        }
    }

    class French : Human
    {
        public override void SayHello()
        {
            Console.WriteLine("Bonjour!");
        }
    }

    class Program
    {
        static void Main(string[] args)
```

```
{
    American a = new American();
    a.SayHello();

    Columbian c = new Columbian();
    c.SayHello();

    French f = new French();
    f.SayHello();

    Console.ReadKey();
  }
 }
}
```

As you can see each class inherits from the Human class and some override the virtual class but some like the American class don't need to override it, this gives the option to changes classes if need be.

Interfaces

Interfaces are very structured, they are a blue print that every inherited method must follow, much like a contract. An interface is much like an abstract class, but how an abstract class should be inherited and possibly extended an interface should just be implemented. Interfaces allow the separation of function definitions from implementation and improves readability and design.

A interface is defined like so, each method or property that is to be created is put in a kind of list, an interface cannot contain any implementation.

```
interface ITransaction
```

```
{
    //Methods
    void Process();
}
```

Below is an example of using an Interface with the example used involving Vehicles:

```
interface IVehicle
{
    string Colour { get; }
    string EngineType { get; }
    int NumberOfWheels { get; }
    int Gas { get; }

    void StartEngine();
    void StopEngine();
}

class Car : IVehicle
{
    public string Colour { get; }
    public string EngineType { get; }
    public int NumberOfWheels { get; } = 4;
    public int Gas { get; }

    public void StartEngine()
    {
        Console.WriteLine("Started Engine!");
    }

    public void StopEngine()
    {
        Console.WriteLine("Stopped Engine!");
    }

    public Car(string colour, string engineType, int gas)
    {
        Colour = colour;
        EngineType = engineType;
        Gas = gas;
    }
```

```
}
```

As you can see, Car has to implement all of the items defined in the IVehicle interface, this gives a kind of "plug and play" effect when creating new classes that relate to Vehicles because the design and layout is strictly enforced.

Exercise

Using the previous example implement a new Class called Bike using the IVehicles Interface, get a feel for how the interface works.

Solution

The implemented class should look like so:

```csharp
class Bike : IVehicle
{
    public string Colour { get; }
    public string EngineType { get; }
    public int NumberOfWheels { get; } = 2;
    public int Gas { get; }

    public void StartEngine()
    {
        Console.WriteLine("Started Engine!");
    }

    public void StopEngine()
    {
        Console.WriteLine("Stopped Engine!");
    }
```

```
    public Bike(string colour, string engineType, int gas)
    {
        Colour = colour;
        EngineType = engineType;
        Gas = gas;
    }
}
```

Namespaces

Namespaces are used to separate definitions, it makes so names defined in one namespace do not clash with another.

A namespace is defined like so:

```
namespace Namespace1
{

}
```

And to call another namespace's function you use the member operator (.), this is done like this:

```
Namespace1.Class c = new Namespace1.Class();
```

Note: Namespaces cannot directly contain functions or variable definitions.

Below is an example of using another namespace:

```csharp
using System;
namespace ConsoleApplication1
{
    class Program
    {
        public class SameName
        {
            public void Function()
            {
                Console.WriteLine("Main!");
            }
        }

        static void Main(string[] args)
        {
            SameName s1 = new SameName();
            s1.Function();

            Namespace1.SameName s2 = new Namespace1.SameName();
            s2.Function();

            Console.ReadKey();
        }
    }
}


namespace Namespace1
{
    public class SameName
    {
        public void Function()
        {
            Console.WriteLine("Namespace1!");
        }
    }
```

```
}
```

Output

>Main!

>Namespace1!

Note how there are two classes with a class with the "SameName" and how you specify which one with the Namespace and the member operator.

Namespaces in other files or this file can be automatically specified by the **using** keyword, you may have noticed the:

```
using System;
```

That has appeared on the top of some of the code snippets, this is basically telling the program to use the "System" namespace for items like:

```
Console.WriteLine("");
```

And

```
Console.ReadKey();
```

Using can also be used to chop off the preceding namespace specifier:

Without the using statement

```
using System;
namespace ConsoleApplication1
{
    class Program
    {
        static void Main(string[] args)
        {
            Namespace1.Class c = new Namespace1.Class();
            c.Function();

            Console.ReadKey();
        }
    }
}

namespace Namespace1
{
    public class Class
    {
        public void Function()
        {
            Console.WriteLine("Namespace1!");
        }
    }
}
```

With the using statement:b

```
using System;
using Namespace1;
namespace ConsoleApplication1
{
```

```
    class Program
    {
        static void Main(string[] args)
        {
            Class c = new Class();
            c.Function();

            Console.ReadKey();
        }
    }
}

namespace Namespace1
{
    public class Class
    {
        public void Function()
        {
            Console.WriteLine("Namespace1!");
        }
    }
}
```

Notice how the Class reference is now shorter and nicer to read.

End of chapter Quiz

1. What are the two main ways of implementing Polymorphism?

2. What is it called when they're more than one versions of a contractor or function?

3. Defining a class as sealed achieves what?

4. What can you not do with an abstract class?

5. What keyword is used when implementing an abstract or virtual method?

6. Namespaces are used for what purpose?

7. Can you create an abstract method that isn't housed in an abstract class?

8. What is the main difference between an Interface and an abstract class?

9. What operator is used when accessing the items of a namespace?

10. How can you tell the complier to include another namespace automatically?

Answers

1. Static and Dynamic polymorphism.

2. Overloading.

3. Means the class cannot be inherited.

4. Directly create an instance of it.

5. Overload.

6. To separate names of classes and methods.

7. No, all abstract methods need to be in an abstract class.

8. Interfaces do not allow implementation to be added and are a blueprint to design new classes.

9. The member operator (full stop).

10. By adding a 'using' statement at the top of the program.

Chapter 4

Intermediate functionality

Operator overloading

C# has support for altering the functionality of many of the built-in operators, such as '+' or the member operator '.' we have come across previously. Operator overloaders are special functions that include the keyword 'operator' followed by the operator sign, exactly like any other function overloaded operators have a return type and parameter list.

In this example, we're going to create a class called 'Grade' and overload the plus operator. An operator overloader is defined like so:

```
public static Grade operator+(Grade a, Grade b)
{

}
```

Note: The operator function needs to be static and public.

The example below implements this overloaded operator:

```
using System;
namespace ConsoleApplication1
{
    class Program
    {
        static void Main(string[] args)
        {
            Grade a = new Grade(30);
```

```csharp
            a.Print();

        Grade b = new Grade(40);
        b.Print();

        Grade c = a + b;
        c.Print();

        Console.ReadKey();
    }
}

class Grade
{
    int mark;

    public Grade(int m)
    {
        mark = m;
    }

    public void Print()
    {
        Console.WriteLine($"The mark is: {mark}", mark);
    }

    public static Grade operator+(Grade a, Grade b)
    {
        Grade c = new Grade(0);
        c.mark = a.mark + b.mark;
        return c;
    }
}
}
```

```
Output

>The mark is: 30

>The mark is: 40

>The mark is: 70
```

The operator in this instance just takes the mark of each grade instance and pluses the result. This is a very basic example and operator overloading can be incredibly useful.

Exercise

So for example if we wanted to compare two grades at the moment if we added:

```
if (a == b)
{
        Console.WriteLine("Equal grades!");
}
```

And set both grades mark to exactly the same, let's say 30. It should print out "Equal grades"

Overload the "==" operator to compare both marks and see if they're equal

Note:

- The operator overload function should return a bool.

- The "!=" Operator also needs to be implemented alongside (This will just do the complete opposite)

Solution

The entire program should look like the example, the new additions are surrounded by the box.

```csharp
using System;
namespace ConsoleApplication1
{
    class Program
    {
        static void Main(string[] args)
        {
            Grade a = new Grade(30);
            a.Print();

            Grade b = new Grade(30);
            b.Print();

            //Test
            if (a == b)
            {
                Console.WriteLine("Equal grades!");
            }

            Console.ReadKey();
        }
    }

    class Grade
    {
        int mark;

        public Grade(int m)
        {
            mark = m;
        }
```

```csharp
public void Print()
{
    Console.WriteLine($"The mark is: {mark}", mark);
}

public static Grade operator+(Grade a, Grade b)
{
    Grade c = new Grade(0);
    c.mark = a.mark + b.mark;
    return c;
}

public static bool operator==(Grade a, Grade b)
{
    return a.mark == b.mark;
}
public static bool operator !=(Grade a, Grade b)
{
    return a.mark != b.mark;
}
    }
}
```

Output

>The mark is: 30

>The mark is: 30

>Equal grades!

Regular expressions

Regular expressions are a way of matching patterns in inputted text, the .NET frame work has a built in regular expression support. This will be an overview of how to use basic expressions, there are a lot of combinations to learn and doing some research after this chapter is advised.

Each regular expression needs to be constructed, below is a list of each character, operator and function that allows you to create a regular expression:

Anchors & Extras

Character	Description
^	Is a reference to the start of the word
$	Refers to the end of a string
\w	Refers to a word consisting of a-z, A-Z, 0-9 and an underscore
+	Refers to 0 or more occurrences
|	Used to specify 'or'
[nnn]	Used to specify a character class to check with, i.e. [abcd] will only ruturn matches on **aabc** and no **dcab**

So for example the regex:

```
^\w+$
```

Looks intimidating I know, but it simply matches any word it is given, using the System.Text.RegularExpression we can match a pattern. The code below demonstrates it:

```csharp
using System;
using System.Text.RegularExpressions;
namespace ConsoleApplication1
{
    class Program
    {
        static void Main(string[] args)
        {
            while (true)
            {
                //Change expression here!
                string regExpression = @"^\w+$";

                Console.WriteLine("Please input text");
                string input = Console.ReadLine();

                if (Regex.IsMatch(input, regExpression))
                {
                    Console.WriteLine($"{input} is a match!", input);
                }
                else
                {
                    Console.WriteLine("No match!");
                }

                Console.WriteLine();
            }

        }
    }
}
```

Copy over this program to a Visual Studio project and run it, try different inputs out. Anything that includes **just** A-Z, a-z, 0-9 and an underscore will match, but spaces and punctuation for example will not return a match.

Note the use of the "@" sign, this is put before a string that want its value to be taken literally, i.e. turning off backslash to specify special characters.

Another more complex example is:

```
^([\w]+\.[\w]+)$
```

The sections in the square brackets specifies the character set, so in this case it's saying any word with (A-Z, a-z, 0-9 and '_') is valid, then it goes onto "\." which checks for a fullstop, and the [\w]+ is repeated again after the stop, so this regex looks for a pattern of a word separated by a full stop. Add this expression to the program used in the previous example and try it out.

This can now be adapted to this complex regex used for identifying email addresses, each section will be explained:

```
^((([\w]+\.[\w]+))|([\w]+))\@([\w]+\.)+([A-Za-z]{1,2}\.([A-Za-z]{1,2})|([A-Za-z]{1,3}))$
```

The regex will now identify email addresses.

- (([\w]+\.[\w]+)|[\w]+))
    - Is equal to any number of standard characters split between with a '.' followed by any number of standard characters
    - OR (|)

59

- o   Any number of standard characters

- \@([\w]+\.)+

  - o   \@ will match just an "@" sign

  - o   Followed by any number of characters

  - o   Followed by a full stop

  - o   + means any number of the items in brackets

- ([A-Za-z]{1,2}\.([A-Za-z]{1,2})|([A-Za-z]{1,3}))

  - o   [A-Za-z] specifies that a word made up of just upper and lower-case letters, the "{1,2}" specifies the length of the word, a minimum of 1 and a max of 2 characters

  - o   \. separated by a '.'

  - o   Another "[A-Za-z]{1,2}"

  - o   OR (|)

  - o   "[A-Za-z]{1,3}" – Same as "[A-Za-z]{1,2}" but with a larger maximum length

Character Escapes

In regular expression, the backslash "\" signify that the character or group of character following it are special or to be taken literally:

Character	Description	Unicode Number (hex)
\t	Will match a tab character	0009
\r	Will match a carriage return (Note this is not the same as a newline (\n)	000D
\f	Matches a form feed (Better known as a page break	000C
\n	Matches a new line	000A
\e	Matches an escape	001B
\nnn	Use octal representation to specify a character (nnn is replaced by values)	Each letter has its own octal
\x nn	Uses a hexadecimal representation to specify a character (nn once again consists of two digits)	Each letter has it's own hexadecimal representation
\unnnn	Uses hexadecimal representation to display a Unicode character, each 'n' is a numeric value	Each Unicode letter has it's own hexadecimal representation
\W	Matches any non-character word	
\s	Matches any whitespace	
\S	Matches any non-whitespace	
\d	Matches any decimal value	
\D	Any character but a decimal value	

Pre-processor directives

Pre-processors directives are designed as messages to the complier, they are processed before any compilation. They are signified by a hash symbol (#) and because of them not being statements do not require and end of line statement (;).

C# pre-processor directives offer nothing different to the ones in C++ or C, and they cannot be used to macros.

Directive	Explination
#define	It creates a symbol
#undef	Used to undefine a symbol
#if	It is used to test a symbol against a condition
#else	Used alongside #if
#elif	And else and an if in the same statement
#endif	Used to signify a close to an #if statement
#line	Modifies the compliers line number and an optional feature is to change file name outputs for files and warnings
#region	Useful for formatting
#endregion	Shows the end of an region

Above is a decently fleshed out table that includes all of the main directives. Below are examples of some useful directives:

#define & #undef & if

The example below shows if #define statement can be used with an #if statement:

```
#define VALUE
using System;
```

```
namespace ConsoleApplication1
{
   class Program
   {
      static void Main(string[] args)
      {
#if (VALUE)
         Console.WriteLine("Defined");
#else
         Console.WriteLine("Not Defined");
#endif
         Console.ReadKey();
      }
   }
}
```

Output
>Defined

As you can tell this can be used to easily toggle code, the most common example is with use with debug code, or a verbose mode:

```csharp
#define VERBOSE
using System;

namespace ConsoleApplication1
{
    class Program
    {
        static void Main(string[] args)
        {
            Console.WriteLine("Start!");

            int a = 1 + 3;
#if (VERBOSE)
            Console.WriteLine("Addition complete");
#endif
            int b = 1 - 4;
#if (VERBOSE)
            Console.WriteLine("Subtraction complete");
#endif

            int c = 1 * 3;
#if (VERBOSE)
            Console.WriteLine("Multiplication complete");
#endif

            int d = 1 / 3;
#if (VERBOSE)
            Console.WriteLine("Division complete");
#endif

            Console.WriteLine("End!");
            Console.ReadKey();
        }
    }
}
```

The example below shows a very basic almost pointless program but it's supposed to demonstrate how #defined can be like toggles, copy over and run the program and compare what the program is like when you add or remove the #define at the top.

#if uses the normal conditionals as an actual if statement, the list is below:

- ==

- || (OR)

- &&

- !=

#region

region offers no purpose to a program when executing but makes it easier to collapse and hide an area of code, it's used like this:

```
#region Hide This
Console.WriteLine("Print!");
#endregion
```

Output

>Print!

When collapsed it will look like this

```
static void Main(string[] args)
{
    Hide This
}
```

Exception Handling

An exception is 'thrown' when an error occurs, it is a response a situation the program cannot continue from. Exceptions can be handled though and your program doesn't have to always explode, there're 4 keywords; **try, catch, finality** and **throw:**

- try – This is used to surround the code you would like to monitor for an exception, if an exception is found it transfers control to the catch section

- catch – This is where the program will end up if an exception is thrown within an accompanying try section.

- finally – This can accompany a try/catch but will run always regardless of an exception being thrown, a good example is when opening a file to read, it always needs closing

- throw – This is used to manually throw an exception with your own custom text.

Below is an example of using a try/catch:

```csharp
using System;

namespace ConsoleApplication1
{
    class Program
    {
        static void Main(string[] args)
        {
            try
            {
                //Diving by zero error!
                int zero = 0;
                int i = 1 / zero;
            }
            catch (Exception e)
            {
                Console.WriteLine(e.Message);
            }
            Console.ReadKey();
        }
    }
}
```

Output

> Attempted to divide by zero.

Note: The highlighted are signifies the parameter for the exception, the exception text can be obtained like below with the ".Message" property. But as you can see the program has printed out the error message, but not thrown a compilation error, the code within the try has not been completed, but has switched to the catch area.

Here is another example but this time a try/catch/finally is being used, this program opens a file (assume it exists) and the finally statement is there to 100% make sure the file is closed even if an exception is thrown.

```csharp
using System;
using System.IO;

namespace ConsoleApplication1
{
    class Program
    {
        static void Main(string[] args)
        {

            StreamReader sr = null;
            try
            {
                sr = new StreamReader("file.txt");

                //Used to simulate an example
                throw new Exception("Error reading file!");
            }
            catch (Exception e)
            {
                Console.WriteLine(e.Message);
            }
            finally
            {
                //Closes the file
                if (sr != null)
                {
```

```
            sr.Close();
        }
    }
        Console.ReadKey();
    }
  }
}
```

Note the use of the "throw new Exception(….." this is used to throw your own custom exceptions, this can be used in situations where you need to be informed of a critical error in your program.

End of chapter Quiz

1. Which key characteristics does an operator overloading function need?

2. What is the role of a regular expression?

3. What is the namespace used for regular expresions?

4. What does putting '@' before a string achieve?

5. How does C#'s directives differ from C or C++?

6. When will a finally statement run?

7. What is the keyword 'throw' used for?

8. What is the role of #region and #endregion?

9. In regular expressions what does "^" signify?

10. In regular expressions, what would this mean [abfe]+

Answers

1. Public and static.

2. Used to match patterns to strings.

3. System.Text.RegularExpressions.

4. It tells the complier to take the string literally and ignore backslash identifiers.

5. There is no support for macros.

6. Always, even if an exception has been thrown.

7. It is used to create your own custom exceptions.

8. They're used for formatting and improved readability.

9. Signifies the start of the word.

10. Any number of characters in a row that are a,b,f and e would be a match

Chapter 5

Program formatting

Attribute

An attribute is a tag used to convey information to the compiler about behaviours of elements of the program, an attribute is specified by a pair of square brackets ([]) and are placed above the element they are providing information about.

The .NET framework provides two types of attribute:

- Predefined

- Custom built

Predefined

There are three pre-defined attribute types:

- AttributeUsage

- Conditional

- Obsolete

Attribute Usage

Attribute usage describes how a custom attribute can be used and where it can be applied, the syntax is below:

```
[AttributeUsage(validOn, AllowMultiple, Inherited)]
```

Where:

- **validOn** specifies where the attribute can be set, it uses the enum "AttributeTargets" that can consist of:

    o AttributeTargets.Class

    o AttributeTargets.Constructor

    o AttributeTargets.Field

    o AttributeTargets.Method

    o AttributeTargets.Property,

- **AllowMultiple** specifies whether more than one version of the attribute can be created and applied.

- **Inherited** specifies whether the attribute is inherited when other classes inherit the attribute the class is connected to

This is used later to make custom attributes.

Conditional

These conditional attributes are used to mark a method that depends on a certain pre-processor directive, this this example we will use a debugging example:

```
using System;
using System.Diagnostics;

namespace ConsoleApplication1
{
    class Program
    {
```

```
    public static void Main()
    {
      Debugging();
      Console.ReadKey();
    }

    [Conditional("DEBUG")]
    static void Debugging()
    {
      Console.WriteLine("This is example debugging code:");
      Console.WriteLine("Number of loops: " + 1);
      Console.WriteLine("Values found: " + 102);
    }
  }
}
```

This will only print out the example output if the program is set in debug mode, this gives a very nice clean way of abstracting code and unnecessary output. The DEBUG flag is automatically built into Visual Studio, so when the program is switched to release mode the debug mode will be false and the code will not run.

This can also be done with custom pre-processor directives like so:

```
#define CUSTOM
using System;
using System.Diagnostics;

namespace ConsoleApplication1
{
    class Program
    {
        public static void Main()
        {
            Custom_Method();
            Console.ReadKey();
        }

        [Conditional("CUSTOM")]
        static void Custom_Method()
        {
            Console.WriteLine("Custom output!");
        }
    }
}
```

Obsolete

This is used for legacy and compatibility reasons, if for example you has a class that used a function SaveFile() but was later updated and this function became obsolete a new function was created called Save() because now this function saved other items, SaveFile() would be marked as obsolete so other programs that use this functions would not have problems with compatibility.

The example shows obsolete being used:

```csharp
using System;

namespace ConsoleApplication1
{
    class Program
    {
        public static void Main()
        {
            Output old = new Output();
            old.PrintData();

            Output newV = new Output();
            newV.Print();

            Console.ReadKey();
        }
    }

    class Output
    {
        string example = "Example";

        [Obsolete("Depreciated! Use Print() instead", false)]
        public void PrintData()
        {
            Console.WriteLine(example);
        }

        public void Print()
        {
            Console.WriteLine(example);
        }
    }
}
```

Output
>Example
>Example

As you can see both method work, however the old.PrintData() will show a warning, it looks like this:

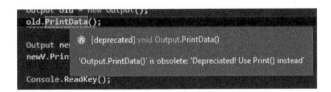

Note: This is because the highlighted 'false' parameter was used, this means just a warning is presented, if this is true an error is created and won't allow the program to compile. This will appear in the error list like this:

Custom Attributes

The framework allows custom created attributes that can store any information the programmer deems relevant information, this is very similar to defining a class, however the class needs to inherit the System.Attribute class, with the AttributeUsage defined above. A basic example is below, the example is definition an attribute that just creates a description:

```
[AttributeUsage(AttributeTargets.Class, AllowMultiple = true, Inherited
= true)]
class Description : Attribute
{
    public string Text { get; }

    public Description(string text)
    {
        Text = text;
    }
}
```

As you can see this is very similar to creating a class, apart from the
inheritance off Attribute and the AttributeUsage attribute above. This can
be used like so:

```
[Description("Main method!")]
[Description("AllowMultiple == true, so you can have multiple
Descriptions")]
class Program
{
    public static void Main()
    {

    }
}
```

This information can be obtained and used by the process of 'reflection',
this will be explored in the next section.

Reflection

Reflection of objects is used for obtaining information at runtime, the System.Reflection gives access to these features.

Reflection can be used to:

- View information about attributes

- It allows late binding to methods and properties

- It allows creation of types at runtime

Metadata

Metadata is data about data, and in this case, it is data about attributes. To start you need to create an instance of Member info like so:

```
MemberInfo info = typeof(AttributeTest);
```

This can now be used to check information. The example below prints off the attributes attached.

Remember to include this at the top

```
using System.Reflection;
```

For the example, we are going to use the Description Attribute from earlier:

```csharp
using System;
using System.Reflection;
namespace ConsoleApplication1
{
    class Program
    {
        static void Main()
        {
            AttributeTest t = new AttributeTest();
            t.PrintAttributes();

            Console.ReadKey();
        }
    }

    [Description("Description 1!")]
    [Description("Description 2!")]
    class AttributeTest
    {
        MemberInfo info = typeof(AttributeTest);

        public void PrintAttributes()
        {
            //Returns an array of attributes
            object[] attributes = info.GetCustomAttributes(true);

            //Prints attributes
            foreach (Description attr in attributes)
            {
                Console.WriteLine(attr.Text);
            }
        }

    }
}
```

```
    [AttributeUsage(AttributeTargets.Class, AllowMultiple = true,
Inherited = true)]
    class Description : Attribute
    {
        public string Text { get; }

        public Description(string text)
        {
            Text = text;
        }
    }
}
```

```
Output
>Description 1!
>Description 2!
```

As you can see the program has printed out the description text from the attributes attached to it. The line:

```
...info.GetCustomAttributes(true);
```

Returns the list of attributes and the attributes are then printed in the following foreach loop.

Indexers

Indexers allow custom classes to be indexed much like you would with an array, each member is accessed with the array access operator ([])

The indexer is defined like so:

```
type this[int index]
{
        get
        {
            //returns values
        }
        set
        {
            //sets values
        }
}
```

Where you would call it like this:

```
Example[2];
```

With the exact syntax on an array.

So, for this example it will be a store inventory searcher, the indexer will take a name and search the catalogue:

```csharp
using System;
using System.Collections.Generic;

namespace ConsoleApplication1
{
    class Program
    {
        static void Main()
        {
            Inventory main_floor = new Inventory();

            //Adds Items
            main_floor.AddItem(new Item("PS4", 499.50));
            main_floor.AddItem(new Item("RX_480", 200.50));

            //Uses indexer to grab price
            Console.WriteLine("Price: " + main_floor["RX_480"]);
            Console.ReadKey();
        }
    }

    class Inventory
    {
        List<Item> Items = new List<Item>();

        public void AddItem(Item item)
        {
            Items.Add(item);
        }

        public double this[string index]
        {
```

```csharp
        get
        {
            foreach (Item item in Items)
            {
                if (item.Name == index)
                {
                    return item.Price;
                }
            }

            //Used to signify that there is not item
            return -1;
        }
        set
        {
            //You can also use this to set a value much like setting a value
in
            //an attribute
        }

    }
}

//Simple class to hold item
class Item
{
    public Item(string name, double price)
    {
        Name = name;
        Price = price;
    }

    public string Name { get; }
    public double Price { get; }
}
}
```

Both the highlighted areas signify where the indexer is defined and used. The program just keeps track of items and the indexer is used to take a string to find the price.

Exercise

Add an overloaded version of the indexer (This can be done) that takes the price as the index and returns the name. For simplicity purposes don't worry about two items having the same price, just assume all items have different prices

Solution

Your Inventory class should look like this: (The new indexer is highlighted)

```
class Inventory
{
    List<Item> Items = new List<Item>();

    public void AddItem(Item item)
    {
        Items.Add(item);
    }

    public double this[string index]
    {
        get
        {
            foreach (Item item in Items)
            {
                if (item.Name == index)
                {
                    return item.Price;
                }
            }


            return -1;
        }
    }
}
```

```csharp
    public string this[double index]
    {
       get
       {
          foreach (Item item in Items)
          {
             if (item.Price == index)
             {
                return item.Name;
             }
          }


          return null;
       }
    }
}
```

Collections

Collection classes are specialized built in classes used for data storage and retrieval. Some of these classes have members that are defined as 'object', object is the base class for all data types in C#. This was the method of storing any data type before the concept of generic classes was implemented.

Below is a list and explanation of the main collections:

List<T>

List is the upgrade more modern version of ArrayList, it is a dynamically sized list that is used to store different values of the same type, it can be extended and reduced (where it resizes automatically). The List class is a generic class (Learned about in the next chapter) but what it means in this case is it can hold anything, even other lists (This is how you can make a 2D list).

A list is defined like so:

```
List<type> list = new List<type>();
```

Where for example a list of integers is defined like so:

```
List<int> list = new List<int>();
```

Values can be added to the list by using the .Add() function and can be removed by using .Remove()

You can obtain the length of the List<> or how many items it houses by accessing the .Count property.

Hashtable

Note: This is depreciated and should not be used, you should use a Dictionary<>, but it's important you know how this collection works.

A hashtable is table (as the name suggests) that stores key-value pairs, these pairs are determined by a hash function. A hash function takes an input of any length and returns a value of fixed length, this process can also no be undone. So in the hashtables case, a keypair that is to be added is hashed, now this hash will be equal to a position in the table. The key pair will then be stored in that location.

Note: the key specified must be unique

One of the biggest positivises of a hashtable is how quick it is to access or check if the table contains and item, this is because in most lineal structures like an array or list you need to incrementally search through a list to exhaustively check if there is an item, but in this case of a hashtable if a search target hashed to find where it would go and there is no value in that location, it's not there.

Dictionary<TKey, TValue>

Must like this List<T>, the Dictionary is a generic data type that is based off the Hashtable mentioned previously is uses a key value pair to save data.

A dictionary is defined like so:

```
Dictionary<KeyType, ValueType> dictionary = new
Dictionary<KeyType, ValueType>();
```

Where "KeyType" and "ValueType" both define the data type that will be used to store each member of the pair.

Adding to the dictionary can be done like so:

```
dictionary.Add(1, "Value");
```

And you can obtain a value by searching for a key:

```
Console.WriteLine(dictionary[key]);
```

And the values can be incremented through using the foreach value, the type that hold both values are called a KeyValuePair<TKey, TValue>. It's done like so:

```
foreach (KeyValuePair<int,string> item in dictionary)
{
        Console.WriteLine(item.Key);
        Console.WriteLine(item.Value);
}
```

Stack

This is known a First-in-Last-out (FILO) data structure where when a value Is placed in its 'pushed' and when a value is taken (Can only be from the top of the stack) it's popped.

A stack Is defined like so:

```
Stack s = new Stack();
```

Values are added buy pushing:

```
s.Push(2);
```

And taken of by popping. Note the use of the integer cast, this is because items are stored as objects.

```
int value = (int)s.Pop();
```

Queue

A Queue is very similar to a stack but instead is a First-in First-out (FIFO) Data structure. Items are added and taken away by using 'Enqueue()' and 'Dequeue()' respectively.

A queue is defined like so:

```
Queue q = new Queue();
```

And adding a removing from a queue is done like so:

```
//Add to the queue
q.Enqueue(1);

//Take from the queue
int i = (int)q.Dequeue();
```

Generics

Generics is a huge feature of C# that allows the programmer to create a single definition of a class that takes any data type, even custom-made classes. The usage of the generic type is denoted by "T", this stems from its origins of originally being called "Templating" in C++. For example the List<> collection we have come across previously is a generic class,

You can create a generic class like so:

```
class Generic<T>
```

```
{

}
```

Notice the uses of <>, these are used to create generic data type, these also do not need to be define as 'T' and can be multiple definitions:

```
class Generic<Example, AnotherExample>
{

}
```

The above example is valid, but it's advised for readability to start the definition with a 'T'. Below is an example how to use the generic data types:

```
class Generic<TEx>
{
    public TEx value;

    public Generic(TEx _value)
    {
        value = _value;
    }

    public void Print()
    {
        Console.WriteLine($"Data is: {value}", value);
    }
}
```

This class definition can be used with any defined data type:

```
Generic<string> gStr = new Generic<string>("Hello");
gStr.Print();

Generic<int> gInt = new Generic<int>(2);
gInt.Print();
```

As you can tell from the code snippet above you define the type to use by definition it in the "<>". In the example below it will show it working with a user defined type:

```
Generic<myClass> gMyClass = new Generic<myClass>(new myClass());
gMyClass.Print();
```

With an output of

```
> Data is: ConsoleApplication1.myClass
```

As you can tell generics allow a very dynamic way of definition a class that allows almost infinite amount of data types. Below is an actual functionally program that is used to swap two data types:

```csharp
using System;
namespace ConsoleApplication1
{
    class Program
    {
        static void Main()
        {
            int a = 10;
            int b = 42;

            Console.WriteLine($"a is before swap: {a}", a);
            Console.WriteLine($"b is before swap: {b}", b);

            Swap<int> swap = new Swap<int>(ref a, ref b);

            Console.WriteLine($"a is after swap: {a}", a);
            Console.WriteLine($"b is after swap: {b}", b);

            Console.ReadKey();
        }
    }
    public class Swap<T>
    {
        public Swap(ref T Left, ref T Right)
        {
            T temp;
            temp = Left;
            Left = Right;
```

```
        Right = temp;
    }
  }
}
```

Another example could be to create a generic array, note the use of indexers to make accessing and changing values easier:

```csharp
using System;
namespace ConsoleApplication1
{
    class Program
    {
        static void Main()
        {
            Array<int> intArray = new Array<int>(1);
            intArray[0] = 1;

            Array<string> strArray = new Array<string>(1);
            strArray[0] = "Hello";

            Console.WriteLine(intArray[0]);
            Console.WriteLine(strArray[0]);
            Console.ReadKey();
        }
    }
    public class Array<T>
    {
        T[] array;
        public Array(int size)
        {
            array = new T[size];
        }

        //Indexer used to access and change values
        public T this[int index]
        {
            get
            {
                return array[index];
            }
            set
```

```
        {
            array[index] = value;
        }
    }

    }
}
```

It's cheating a little bit to have an array internally defined but you get the picture. The array is defined as an array of generics, this allows for a type to be defined later on.

End of chapter Quiz

1. What are the two types of attributes that the .NET Framework supports?

2. Where would you normally find the Obsolete built in attribute?

3. When creating a custom attribute, which class does it need to inherit?

4. How would you define 'metadata'?

5. What is the role of reflection in code?

6. What method can be used to get attribute info on a function?

7. What's the biggest reason to use an indexer?

8. When referring to a stack what does FIFO?

9. What brackets signify a generic class?

10. What variable is used to save the key and value of a dictionary?

Answers

1. Predefined and custom built.

2. On old deprecated method that can't be removed due to compatibility reasons but needs to be phased out.

3. System.Attribute.

4. Data about data.

5. View the underlying data of function or property.

6. GetCustomAttributes()

7. Improve syntax when accessing or changing values in a class.

8. First-in First-out.

9. < and >, inside the brackets the generic types are defined.

10. KeyValuePair<TKey, TValue>

Chapter 6

Processes and functionality

Delegates

Delegates are very similar to function pointers in C or C++ if you have come across this concept before. So, delegates are a reference type variable that holds references to a function.

A real-world use for delegates is using them for dynamic calls back to a function, the delegate is passed as a parameter and the function is dynamically called.

So for example the definition below can be used to reference any method that has two int parameters, it returns an integer and is marked as private.

public delegate int ExampleDeligate(int a, int b);

You then would create an instance of this delegate by using the 'new' keyword like so:

```
using System;
namespace ConsoleApplication1
{
    class Program
    {
        public delegate int ExampleDeligate(int a, int b);
        static void Main()
        {
```

```
        ExampleDeligate addDel = new
ExampleDeligate(AddTwoNumbers);
    }

    public static int AddTwoNumbers(int a, int b)
    {
        return a + b;
    }
  }
}
```

As you can see the delegate is initialised and in the brackets is the name of function it will reference.

To use the delegate just treat it as it like any other function:

```
addDel(1, 2);
```

This gives a nice dynamic, useable way to pass functions as parameters. Below is an example using this to act as a calculator;

```
using System;
namespace ConsoleApplication1
{
  class Program
  {
    public delegate float Calculation(float a, float b);
    static void Main()
    {
        //All you have to do is pass in the function by name
        Calculater(10, 20, Add);
```

```csharp
            Calculater(5, 267, Sub);
            Calculater(14, 2, Mul);
            Calculater(10, 10, Div);

            Console.ReadKey();
        }

        public static void Calculater(float a, float b, Calculation cal)
        {
            //Dynamic method call
            float value = cal(a, b);
            Console.WriteLine($"New value is: {value}", value);
        }


        //Basic functions
        public static float Add(float a, float b)
        {
            return a + b;
        }
        public static float Sub(float a, float b)
        {
            return a - b;
        }
        public static float Mul(float a, float b)
        {
            return a * b;
        }
        public static float Div(float a, float b)
        {
            return a / b;
        }
    }
}
```

The highlighted area shows how you can pass in a delegate as a parameter, and all you do is pass in the function in the delegates parameter position, this gives a wonderfully easy dynamic way to reuse code.

Multicasting

Delegates also allow the concatenation of function calls onto each other, like this:

```
Calculation DEL = new Calculation(Add);
DEL += new Calculation(Sub);
DEL += new Calculation(Mul);
DEL += new Calculation(Div);
```

This means all the method will be called in one long chain, so for example say the parameters are 10 and 20 the answer would be equal to the last method added, in this case (10/20 = 0.5), in this example it runs over all the method but they don't affect each other so it doesn't change the answer, so careful consideration Is needed when choosing what method to add to a multicast delegate.

But the new example below it should multicasting when not returning values:

```csharp
using System;
namespace ConsoleApplication1
{
    class Program
    {
        public delegate void Print();
        static void Main()
        {
            Print call = new Print(PrintHello);
            call += new Print(PrintToday);
            call += new Print(PrintCar);

            //Method call
            call();

            Console.ReadKey();
        }

        public static void PrintHello()
        {
            Console.WriteLine("Hello");
        }
        public static void PrintToday()
        {
            Console.WriteLine("Today");
        }
        public static void PrintCar()
        {
            Console.WriteLine("Car");
        }
    }
}
```

This shows you can string multiple function calls into one delegate call, this can also be passed as a parameter and used in another function.

Anonymous Methods

Previously we mentioned previously delegates are used to reference any methods with the same signature as the delegate.

Anonymous methods provide a technique to pass a code block as a delegate parameter. They're methods without a name, so there're just the body. You do not need to define the return type of the method, it's inferred (automatically determined) from the return statement in the methods body.

They are effectively delegates that aren't referencing an actual method, it's being created just for the delegate, so going back to our calculator example it would look like this:

```
using System;
namespace ConsoleApplication1
{
    //Delegate
    public delegate int Calculation(int a, int b);

    class Program
    {
        Calculation add = delegate (int a, int b)
        {
            return a + b;
        };
        Calculation sub = delegate (int a, int b)
        {
            return a - b;
        };
        Calculation mul = delegate (int a, int b)
        {
            return a * b;
        };
        Calculation div = delegate (int a, int b)
        {
            return a / b;
        };

        static void Main()
        {
            Program p = new Program();

            p.add(10, 20);
```

```
    p.div(2, 10);

    Console.WriteLine();
  }
 }
}
```

Where each command is defined as an anon method, and just called like a regular function.

The use of anonymous methods reduces the coding overhead of creating delegates because another method does not need defining prior to creating a delegate instance.

method seems wasteful.

So anonymous methods should be used when the overhead of creating a

Events

Events are user actions such as key pressed, clicks, mouse movements etc. This allows programs or code to execute that is dependent on an event triggering, this is known as event-driven programming.

Delegates are often used with events, events are associated with the event handler (trigger detection) by using the delegate. Events use the publisher-subscriber model:

- A publisher is a class that contains the event, this is as the name suggests used to publish the event.

- The subscriber class is a class that accepts the event. The delegate in the publisher class invokes the method of the subscriber class.

Declaring Event

To declare an event internally in a class, you first need a delegate type defined and attach it to the handler. The code below demonstrates this:

```
using System;
namespace ConsoleApplication1
{
    //Delegate
    public delegate string DelExample(string str);

    class EventExample
    {
        //Event decleration
        event DelExample MyEvent;

        public EventExample()
        {
            MyEvent += new DelExample(PrintWelcome);
        }

        public string PrintWelcome(string username)
        {
            return username + " Welcome!";
        }

        static void Main()
        {
            EventExample ex = new EventExample();

            //Calls the event handler
            Console.WriteLine(ex.MyEvent("User1"));
            Console.ReadKey();
        }
    }
}
```

Multithreading

A thread is a single process of execution, multithreading is the ability to run lots of small processes concurrently (At the same time), this stops programs from wasting CPU cycles waiting and can make programs much more efficient.

However, introducing multithreading into problems that are trivial or cannot be run concurrently can add an unnecessary overhead and can reduce the efficiency of a program.

So far we have written programs that execute in a single thread and the computer executes them just from start to finish in one straight line.

Threads

The tools required to create and work with threads resides in the System.Threading class. One of the simplest functions is being able to grab the current thread, this is done like so:

```
Thread t = Thread.CurrentThread;
```

Creating Threads

You can create a thread like so:

```
Thread s = new Thread(DoLotsOfWork);
```

With the function the thread will executing being contained in the brackets. The example below shows how this concurrent behaviour can work:

```csharp
using System;
using System.Threading;

namespace ConsoleApplication1
{
    class Program
    {
        public static void DoLotsOfWork()
        {
            for (int i = 0; i < 5; i++)
            {
                Thread t = Thread.CurrentThread;
                Console.WriteLine($"{t.Name}: i is equal to: {i}");
            }
        }

        static void Main()
        {
            for (int i = 0; i < 5; i++)
            {
                //Creates a thread
                Thread s = new Thread(DoLotsOfWork);

                //Assigns the thread a name
                s.Name = $"Thread {i}";

                s.Start();
            }

            Console.ReadKey();
        }
    }
}
```

Output

```
>Thread 2: i is equal to: 0

>Thread 2: i is equal to: 1

>Thread 2: i is equal to: 2

>Thread 2: i is equal to: 3

>Thread 2: i is equal to: 4

>Thread 0: i is equal to: 0

>Thread 1: i is equal to: 0

>Thread 0: i is equal to: 1

>Thread 1: i is equal to: 1

>Thread 1: i is equal to: 2

>Thread 1: i is equal to: 3

>Thread 1: i is equal to: 4

>Thread 0: i is equal to: 2

>Thread 0: i is equal to: 3

>Thread 0: i is equal to: 4

>Thread 3: i is equal to: 0

>Thread 3: i is equal to: 1

>Thread 3: i is equal to: 2

>Thread 3: i is equal to: 3

>Thread 3: i is equal to: 4

>Thread 4: i is equal to: 0

>Thread 4: i is equal to: 1

>Thread 4: i is equal to: 2
```

```
>Thread 4: i is equal to: 3

>Thread 4: i is equal to: 4
```

Note: this may come through in a different order for you.

This example above creates 5 threads that prints out 5 iterations of a for loop, as you can see it doesn't all come through in order, this is because it's occurring concurrently and each of these threads are working independently.

This lack of order can be a problem in some circumstances, this is where the "lock" keyword comes into its own, it's used to surround code that is deemed crucial and code that cannot have multiple threads using it at the same time, we'll adapt the example from before to include the lock:

```csharp
using System;
using System.Threading;

namespace ConsoleApplication1
{
    class Program
    {
        static object padLock = new object();
        public static void DoLotsOfWork()
        {
            lock (padLock)
            {
                for (int i = 0; i < 5; i++)
                {

                    Thread t = Thread.CurrentThread;
                    Console.WriteLine($"{t.Name}: i is equal to: {i}");

                }
```

```
        }
    }

    static void Main()
    {
        for (int i = 0; i < 5; i++)
        {
            //Creates a thread
            Thread s = new Thread(DoLotsOfWork);

            //Assigns the thread a name
            s.Name = $"Thread {i}";

            s.Start();
        }

        Console.ReadKey();
    }
}
}
```

Output
>Thread 0: i is equal to: 0
>Thread 0: i is equal to: 1
>Thread 0: i is equal to: 2
>Thread 0: i is equal to: 3
>Thread 0: i is equal to: 4
>Thread 2: i is equal to: 0
>Thread 2: i is equal to: 1
>Thread 2: i is equal to: 2

```
>Thread 2: i is equal to: 3

>Thread 2: i is equal to: 4

>Thread 1: i is equal to: 0

>Thread 1: i is equal to: 1

>Thread 1: i is equal to: 2

>Thread 1: i is equal to: 3

>Thread 1: i is equal to: 4

>Thread 3: i is equal to: 0

>Thread 3: i is equal to: 1

>Thread 3: i is equal to: 2

>Thread 3: i is equal to: 3

>Thread 3: i is equal to: 4

>Thread 4: i is equal to: 0

>Thread 4: i is equal to: 1

>Thread 4: i is equal to: 2

>Thread 4: i is equal to: 3

>Thread 4: i is equal to: 4
```

As you can see each iteration loop is coming through in order, i.e. from 0 – 4, may also be able to see that the threads are not necessarily in order, the lock works on a first come first serve basic and once a thread touches it, it becomes locked until the object is released. Please also not the use of an object alongside the lock, this is used as a flag for if the lock is available or locked.

This lock system is very useful when it comes to dealing with files, if two threads were to try and read or write to a file at the same time there will be errors or lines would not appear in order. Below is an example demoing this:

```csharp
using System;
using System.IO;
using System.Threading;

namespace ConsoleApplication1
{
    class Program
    {
        public static void WriteToFile()
        {
            //Error here!
            StreamWriter sw = new StreamWriter("file.txt");
            for (int i = 0; i < 5; i++)
            {
                sw.WriteLine($"Test {i}");
            }
            sw.Close();
        }

        static void Main()
        {
            for (int i = 0; i < 5; i++)
            {
                //Creates a thread
                Thread s = new Thread(WriteToFile);

                //Assigns the thread a name
                s.Name = $"Thread {i}";

                s.Start();
            }

            Console.ReadKey();
        }
    }
}
```

```
}
```

This will crash and throw a **System.IO.IOException** as two or more threads will try and open the file to write to it at the same time. This is a real-world usage for the lock structure as adding a lock will solve this, below is the lock being introduced, this will solve the issue:

```csharp
using System;
using System.IO;
using System.Threading;

namespace ConsoleApplication1
{
    class Program
    {
        static object padLock = new object();
        public static void WriteToFile()
        {
            lock (padLock)
            {
                StreamWriter sw = new StreamWriter("file.txt");
                for (int i = 0; i < 5; i++)
                {
                    sw.WriteLine($"Test {i}");
                }
                sw.Close();
                Console.WriteLine("File written to!");
            }
        }

        static void Main()
        {
            for (int i = 0; i < 5; i++)
            {
```

```
        //Creates a thread
        Thread s = new Thread(WriteToFile);

        //Assigns the thread a name
        s.Name = $"Thread {i}";

        s.Start();
    }

    Console.ReadKey();
  }
 }
}
```

This code will now not crash, but it really cannot be considered multithreaded, it used multiple threads but effectively acts as a single threaded application, the lock statement should only be used when it's entirely necessary. Copy this code over and have a play with it and get familiar with how this code works.

LINQ

LINQ stands for Language Integrated Query and solves the problems with querying data and allows a tight readable compact syntax for returning queries from data.

We'll only be covering the LINQ queries for internal objects, but LINQ can be used to query data represented in many different ways. The diverse ways are:

- LINQ to objects

- LINQ to XML

- LINQ to datasets

- LINQ to SQL (DLINQ)

- LINQ to entities

There are two types of syntax for LINQ:

- Lambda (Method) Syntax:

```
var longWords = words.Where(w => w.Length > 10);
```

- Query (Compression) Syntax

```
var longWords = from w in words where w.Length > 10 select
w;
```

We'll only go into the query syntax because I think it's the easiest to use but feel free to take a look at the other query for extra research.

Query Syntax

The query syntax is just a representation comparable to that of SQL, with a SELECT, FROM and WHERE represented in slightly different representation. To use LINQ queries, you need to include System.linq. Below is an example of using LINQ to search through some strings for values with less than 5 letters:

```
using System;
using System.Linq;
```

```
namespace ConsoleApplication1
{
    class Program
    {
        static void Main()
        {
            string[] words = {"test","verylongword", "sw", "one"};

            var shortWords = from word in words
                        where word.Length < 5
                        select word;

            foreach (var word in shortWords)
            {
                Console.WriteLine(word);
            }
            Console.ReadKey();
        }
    }
}
```

Output
>test
>sw
>one

The LINQ statement is highlighted and will be broken down:

from word in words

This defines the range and where the range is from, this is effectively saying every word in the string array 'words'

where word.Length < 5

Using the range value word, it grabs a property and compares it to a value, this is a conditional where if a value matches as 'true' will be added to the output.

```
select word;
```

If the previous conational was true, this is the value to take, so for example you could return the lengths of all words under 5 values by saying at the end of the query:

```
select word.Length;
```

Exercise

In the skeleton program below, add a LINQ statement to search through the array of values 'numbers' to search for even numbers. Then use a foreach loop to print the resulth

Code

```
using System;
using System.Linq;

namespace ConsoleApplication1
{
    class Program
    {
        static void Main()
        {
            int[] numbers = {1, 4, 99, 34, 23, 12, 3, 2, 909, 1000, 13, 1, 2};

            //Add code goes here

            Console.ReadKey();

        }
    }
}
```

Solution

```
using System;
using System.Linq;

namespace ConsoleApplication1
```

```
{
    class Program
    {
        static void Main()
        {
            int[] numbers = {1,4,99, 34, 23, 12, 3, 2, 909, 1000, 13, 1, 2};

            var evenNumbers = from value in numbers
                              where value % 2 == 0
                              select value;

            foreach (var value in evenNumbers)
            {
                Console.WriteLine(value);
            }
            Console.ReadKey();
        }
    }
}
```

The output should also be:

```
>4
>34
>12
>2
>1000
>2
```

So, remember LINQ offers a very nice tight controlled syntax for looking through data, it can also be used to look through many types of data

122

including running SQL commands on a database to query data in tables that can be incredibly powerful for a programmer.

End of chapter Quiz

1. What do delegates allow a programmer to do?

2. What does multicasting allow you to do with delegates?

3. What is an anonymous method?

4. What is an event handler attached to?

5. What is a thread?

6. What is the structure called that prevents two threads from using the same block of code?

7. What does LINQ stand for?

8. What does LINQ allow you to do?

9. What are the two types of syntax for LINQ?

10. In what scenario would multithreading now help?

Answers

1. Save a reference to a function, this allows the programmer to pass function calls around as parameters.

2. You can squash many functions calls into a single delegate.

3. A function without the function definition and is just a delegate defined with a body.

4. A delegate that fires when the event is triggered.

5. A single independent process of execution.

6. Lock.

7. Language Integrated Query

8. Quickly query data for results, for example if you just wanted words with a length of 5 characters.

9. Query and Lambda.

10. When the problem is trivial i.e. a simple problem.

www.ingramcontent.com/pod-product-compliance
Lightning Source LLC
LaVergne TN
LVHW052302060326
832902LV00021B/3674